PRAISE FOR MICHAEL

"*Michael Garrigan is a poet who writes on the water. You can smell the river in his lines, feel the scales on your palms.*"

—NOAH DAVIS, *Anglers Journal*

"*A disciple of ecology, diligent with accuracy, as though to name is to accept responsibility for it: he identifies not just what he loves at first sight, but also what he has grown to love.*"

—ANGELA DRIBBEN, *Revolute*

"*He...is an outdoorsman and knows that nature is our most challenging companion....He worships water and treasures native brook trout that manage to survive in a realm of culm banks, invasive knotweed, dead ash, and dying hemlock. The woods, his fine poems suggest, are all we have, all we ever had.*"

—CHRIS CAMUTO, *Gray's Sporting Journal*

"*This storyteller is a fisherman, telling much more than fish stories. His connection to the space around him explores universal questions of life and death and the hereafter.*"

—TYLER TRUMAN JULIAN, *The Shore*

RIVER, AMEN

RIVER, AMEN

POEMS BY

MICHAEL GARRIGAN

WAYFARER BOOKS
BERKSHIRE MOUNTAINS, MASSACHUSETTS

All Rights Reserved
Published in 2023 by Wayfarer Books
Cover Design and Interior Design by Leslie M. Browning
Cover Image © Levi Bare
TRADE PAPERBACK 978-1-956368-37-6

10 9 8 7 6 5 4 3 2 1

Look for our titles in paperback, ebook, and audiobook wherever books are sold.
Wholesale offerings for retailers available through Ingram.

Wayfarer Books is committed to ecological stewardship.
We greatly value the natural environment and invest in conservation.
For each book purchased in our online store we plant one tree.

PO Box 1601, Northampton, MA 01060

860.574.5847   info@homeboundpublications.com

HOMEBOUNDPUBLICATIONS.COM & WAYFARERBOOKS.ORG

ALSO BY MICHAEL GARRIGAN

Robbing the Pillars

Songenizios (chapbook co-written with Andrew Jones)

What I Know [How to Do] (chapbook)

For the Allweins and Shirks,
For the Garrigans and Augustines

For Jess and For You,
Always

CONTENTS

II - RIVERLAND HYMNS

III - BLOOD & BARK

IV · CONCLUDING RITES

Maybe the problem is that I got involved with the wrong crowd
of gods when I was seven.

—JIM HARRISON

CREATION STORY

Psalms of Ravines

River birch and rhododendrons
        hemlocks and heartaches of lost fish,
Fall in love with river bends
        because they always bend again.

Cup life like boulders hold soft
        pockets of water and when waking,
let it be like gentle licks of fir needles
        on the underside of deer hooves.

Walk back and forth to water, trample a path to follow.

Incantations of Rust

When bones are stripped of skin
trace the minute fissures that mark
vibrations of trains rolling the rails of our days.
        Search maps for blue lines and hash marks
        following the slow topography of rivers' decisions,
        Go there. Listen for songs of iron and skunk cabbage.
           Find bones rusting clean.

Mantras of Rivers

Each river becomes a prayer,
        an act of devotion to the constant
roil and calm movement and stillness.
        Stand naked in water, honest, genuflect
casts across currents, kneel on moss-skinned
        rock altars. The river sings most beautifully
when you are there to listen. Listen before
        all these water songs evaporate.

I - UNLATCHING

Refuse the old means of measurement.
Rely instead on the thrumming
wilderness of self. Listen.
  —Donika Kelly

OF BLOOD AND BARK

Some are born of blood
Some are born of bark.

Some press their chest
against trees until
they bleed into heartwood
          —beat to beat—

Some wander across
hills and down ravines
so when what pulses in veins
spills it mixes well with soil,
sucked up by mycelium
          —vein to vein—
and eventually finds its way
into the genetics of the forest.

          —A grafting of blood and bark—

COMMUNION

Take these wafers of jewelweed
and ragweed between fingers
place them on your tongue, now say
      Father Son Holy Ghost
      (forehead stomach shoulders)
      Swallow. Amen.

You are now a humid summer day,
veins of thicket creepers spread through you,
your eyebrows are crows, your eyes eagles,
your feet stay feet, but now leave
paw prints of five in the mud, river otters.
Your knees don't bend, they arch, elderberry.
Your lips do not kiss but stab deadwood
resting on railroad bed gravel searching for ants,
splintering the afternoon, finding shade.

LISTENIN' TO CHARLIE PARR WHILE WATCHING THE SUNSET OVER THE MIDDLE FORK OF THE FLATHEAD RIVER

The clouds are slow, rain still clings to pine needles,
a white-tailed deer scours the far shore for aster seed.

> The river has barely lifted
>   Rocks stay dry.

The woods are green crayon smeared on tabletop,
dry crumbles flaking off in hushes become fog.

> We are darkness. We are slow
> acoustic slides across taut strings,
>   *Our hands our feet our hearts*

We are dirt roads walked on by few shoes, rutted by few cars.
We are scampering up steep scree slopes towards safety, shelter,

towards meadow-warmth and the last pink light scattering
into Cassiopeia's crutched elbows, sound in their tight bend.

> We are strumming fading notes
> and bending rhythms into lives,
>   *ain't they all the same*

COAL COUNTRY PARADISE
Centralia, PA

The graffiti highway cratered with smoke potholes
knuckles through a town turned graveyard back in '62.
Snow lines ridges, the Main Street crease stays
clear from a constant heat pulse. 120 over 80, steady.

We fade in ash of iron stains and sulfur
tattoos falling from subterranean fires,
an industrial afterlife of fractured asphalt,
bleeding orange mountain veins.

A new world will grow from our collapse into a coal country paradise
as we slowly compress into a new geological layer. Maybe, in a few
thousand years, they will find our fossils and conjecture that we lived
in the dark eating Styrofoam, breathing coal smoke and drinking
water from traffic cones, our bones bent to our faces as we fell
in love with the acidic elixir of silica benzene and mercury.

FROZEN VERMONT POND AUBADE

The farmer wakes in the dark to a cooling wood stove
and hears his cows' long lows as he laces his leather

boots. He doesn't have time to watch the full moon slide
into the crescent thaw on the pond but if he did he'd think

about the warmth of his wife under their wool
comforter and their dog that is now curled next

to his pillow, lingering in the sleep heat he just gave
and how maybe this is all there is to these short days

between Christmas and New Years and snow thawing
in the slight sunlight of this hillside but instead his mind

turns to the deer parts they found on their walk yesterday freezing
to the ground, a clean-cut head lying almost propped at the base

of a sugar maple, eyes exposed, staring at its dismembered sour
torso, legs scattered in the snow. Coyotes? A poacher? A truck?

He yanked their dog back from searching for the sweet
warmth that must lie in the deepest part of the body.

Maybe this is our nature—soil and skin drawn towards
sweet and sour, freezing and thawing, wool and leather.

SKINNING A GROUNDHOG
for Erik

Killed while short-strut loping across a field with birdshot from my bolt action
single-shot twenty-two just four steps from the shed, I know I'll have to clean out
all those damn pellets, carving just a bit into skin with the tip of my black handled
skinning knife; but it's the shot I got and we want a stew this weekend. Laid
back, legs tied to plywood, just enough pressure against the bristled fur down the
centerline stomach seam pulls meat from skin, spreading separating and stretching
brown into a charred red hide I roll as the knife slips around his legs and shoulder
until all I have is taut meat and the underside of skin.

Another unlatching when the abdomen opens.

I pull out the viscera and the body deflates into meat and tendon and bone. When
released it's all we have left. Meat, tendon, bone. I break the ribcage to get to the
heart and lungs—lungs for sausage filler, heart for the dog. The last bones break with
wrist pressure and cleaver clack and spine separates at vertebrae and feet at ankles.
This is the hard part, the search for the scent glands so they don't stink up the stew,
each one just a bit bigger than birdshot; once they're thrown in the grass I submerge
the whole body into the pot and let it soak in salt water overnight, praying the salt
burns away the pain it died with, that pain we carry with us waiting for the last
unlatching.

WHEN HE WAS A BOY

What is it like? he asks her.
She just touches and he knows.

Life is simple like that.
    Touching and knowing.
        Seeing and hearing.

Just yesterday he watched a fox
run-pounce onto a mole burrowing
in soil under a foot of snow.

    He listened. He waited.

LITURGY OF BECOMING
A RIVER LOVING SPIRITUAL SKEPTIC

I bind blankets of poached deer hide
    with 5x tippet in weaving dirt road
patterns and lay them down in the bed
    of my truck to sleep easy under a moon
loping along a valley of public forest lands.
    I dip my index and middle fingers in railroad
grease and smear old industry under my eyes
    to blunt the blinking glare of fracking well pad lights,
those false corporate gods. This helps me sleep.
    I suck ferric hydroxide from tainted streams
and let brown trout slip out of my hands
    before crossing myself in the name
of our fathers, mothers, the lineages lost
    under rock that this river still bleeds.
I map my life line in a palm full of dead
    mayflies, always leading to another crease
in this hard earth as I hum hymns in harmony
    with spring peepers, cicadas, and hellbenders.
I scavenge ravines for shafts of fleeting light
    painting dark water with bloodroot shadows,
waiting for skirts to lift off canopies of Tulip Poplar
    and Hemlock, for trout to rise to a Parachute Adams.
I pray on riparian pews and kneelers of lichen
    crawling across sandstone of eroding
mountains and vermiculating horizons
    of stars I name with whiskey sips. My faith
built on headwaters and confluences, I bless
    myself in the stoups of wild watersheds.

UPON HEARING THAT SNAKEHEAD CATFISH PASSED THROUGH THE CONOWINGO DAM FISH LADDER

I can't help thinking about the shad that struggled to find that ladder trying to spread their seed upstream and how amazing it would have been to see silver schools running up river clogging mouths of small streams each spring tumbling and tangling right under the surface, sometimes breaking through like coils of chrome holding all the tension of a spring pushed down bursting apart into river waves crashing against dolomite boulders sandstone cobbles zigzag rocks and those long thin slices of shale. A convergence of geology and germination. Maybe when they slowed you could see yourself in them, concave hubcap mirrors pulling skin taut like a caudal fin. Maybe these trees still have DNA deep in their rings from rotting shad spawned out left lying for heron eagles osprey. Each year fewer and fewer make it up that ladder. Dwindling decomposition stuck behind a wall, shad flakes glittering Conowingo Dam concrete. This spring Snakehead Catfish finally passed through, finding that ladder easily in just a few years after scouring their way through the Chesapeake Bay, eating everything they could. Some say they can crawl across land.

Maybe the shad are just like these mountains—growing old, eroding into riverbed. Soon this will all be a long valley. Eelgrass gone from yearly floods, Snakeheads gathering in deep pools behind dams, Channel and Flatheads spreading up through riffles where water moves. Some smallmouth bass and carp hovering around island shallows. Even they were once invasive. We all were. Except those shad. A catfish river. That's what this water has become—an ecosystem of non-native invasive species, holding what's left of us.

LEARNING TO SPEY CAST

I've been making these motions
my whole life unknowingly
     lifting levering my arms
     sweeping slowing down.

As a child I swung hands
arcing across air until they,
palm to palm thumb to thumb,
formed a mountain with fingertip peaks,
     prayers bundled at feet running
     lines through current.

As a teenager, arms snapped apart,
              one back behind shoulder
     one held tight to stomach,
before shooting forward for the far side
     looking for that quick violent bite
     from the darkness of the undercut bank.

Here in my 30's I finally let line
go tight and swing slowly through runs, rod
     balanced in hand,
waiting for the subtle strike of downstream deities
knowing that most casts have no answer

WEST COAST INNER STATES SONGENIZIO

on a line from Arbouretum's "Oceans Don't Sing"

Statements and plans that were made, passing by
as we drive, stateless, borderless, homeless
up and down this Pacific cradled state,
we fall into ditch kingdoms. Apostates
we have become, thieving these wild estates
traversing burnt interstates slicing through
fault lines, wineries, and understated
smog sunsets. We devastate the inside
of our old forms, a new state of being
that gestates in our beards and granola.
Statements scratched in sand, silent prayers to
Joshua Tree crucifixions substrates
of full moon oceans. Here is our new state,
a statement of calling, a song of fate.

For Andrew Jones

WHY THE POET FISHES
A BLACK WOOLLY BUGGER HAIBUN

He once tied on a bright pink egg and carried his old eight and a half foot six
weight Winston up a tributary to Cayuga Lake when he should have been throwing
streamers so he could feel the whole reach of that rod but he heard the salmon had
possibly started running, finding their prespawn homes, and with only two hours
to explore and last night's sleet still matting down all the hart's tongue ferns and
roundleaf sundews it felt like the right thing to do and as the sun came out and
he parked his truck he watched two guys pull out a gigantic brown, their hands
reaching into its gills, blood licking their arms so he kept walking and walking,
upstream, upstream until the creek made a big bend and in that dark curve there
was a tree sunken along the far bank so he flicked the fly into the head of the run
and it sank and he pulled in some line to let it drift just right and it sank a bit more
and then it stalled and it was caught and he yanked, thinking it was a rock since it
didn't move, so he yanked again, and it finally moved just a nudge and so he yanked
again, thinking he could free it and luckily he was wrong and I know you've heard
this before, but on that next yank it yanked back and bent the rod completely, fully,
into a tight crescent bridge between flesh and water and now he was high stepping
it downstream as whatever wasn't a rock coursed downstream and so he followed
it, trying to push the fish into some shallow water since it was too deep for him to
wade any closer and each time, each-fucking-time it was close it would turn and
shoot back upstream to the head of the run and they went back and forth like this
for about ten minutes— downstream then upstream, downstream then upstream,
a pendulum of desire to reach and to escape—until, finally, the fish tired out at the
tail of the pool and he got close enough to net it but his net was too small because
he usually only catches small native brook trout and wild browns that might
occasionally reach eighteen inches and someone somehow suddenly appeared behind
him with a big black nylon net and handed it to him and he finally landed the fish
and they high fived and whooped and shared in those wordless joyful moments

of catharsis when all that pent up air in you leaves in guttural punches breaking
through the meniscus of this world and as he went to release the landlocked salmon,
all 26 inches of it, he found a big black conehead woolly bugger notched in its upper
lip, a couple of inches of 8 lb mono still dangling from the eyelet, and he took that
bugger and now he looks at it as he writes and that salmon is always here, in this
room with him, nestled under that sunken log, sucking down brown trout eggs,
building its redds, waiting until spring comes to go back into the deep lake and the
poet keeps writing, trying to map that hidden landscape, trying to find a way back
to her.

Each river swallows
everything, keeping hidden
what we are called to.

SEARCHING THE DATABASE
OF PRIESTS ACCUSED OF SEXUAL ASSAULT

Monsignor would place the cloth he dried his hands
       with, veins stretched from his wrist under faint
       gray hairs after I poured water over them
       before blessing the Eucharist, our backs
       to the Congregation, the altar at our waist,
into my hands,
       palms open, waiting, and squeeze
       them shut in what I always imagined
       as a secret handshake as water seeped
       through my fingers into the lavabo bowl
       with each contraction of muscle.

Years after my last genuflection searching
through hundreds of names on a list, next to his
       —photos of nude altar boys, dismissed, deceased—

What if all we have are paintings of the Last Supper?
What if transubstantiation is just a manipulation of the sacred to the profane,
a simple squeeze of faith? What if that wafer is still dry, stuck to my gums,
and that cloth still wet, clumped in my palm, dripping through my fingers?

Or what if, what if he loved me for waking up early every Sunday
and ringing those bells at just the right time, his arms held high,
for kneeling, back straight, still, during the Eucharistic Prayer?

What if we didn't have to ask, but just receive
these holy unblemished gifts of the bounty?

DEER TRAILS

Always seem
to find the
quickest
way to water
with the least
amount of thorns
and it feels good
to stand where
they kneel
to drink
and I hope
my scent
doesn't
ruin
it.

DEAD WATER DEITIES

I hike rails deep into a cold hollow crease of the Kittatinny Ridge
where I build a railbed-gravel fire, warming plunge pool psalms
of cloudy sunset stains as trout shoot under crumbling ledges.

> I pray to dead water deities,
> water gods lost to coal and pyrite
> returning and reclaiming this rusted ravine.

Deadwood burns light and heat into ash
like these hills once flamed and smoked as
machines gouged and scraped a landscape interrupted.
> Woods sing ballads of bones creaking
> in rivers and saints butchered under floods.

Fires die floods recede, but the rhythms of these rails
and abandoned totems gather into eddies of song,
> chants for the gods of a new world,
> native brook trout that survived in headwaters,
> wild browns that have migrated from big rivers,
> the seeds of a rewilding.

7TH ANTHRACITE COAL DISTRICT OF PENNSYLVANIA

The Lord gives us mountains
and we fail to mine out that grandness
      –Anders Carlson-Wee

Victor Augustine was declared competent to be a miner
in the Seventh Anthracite Coal District Mines of this great
Commonwealth on the 20th day of May 1905.

Twenty years later, just before his death under dark rock,
his son Albert Augustine was declared competent to be a miner
in this great Commonwealth on the 20th Day of June 1925.

I met Albert, Poppy, as he was dying. Something with his lungs,
dark rock slowly collapsing onto him from inside each of his breaths.
Poppy was the last miner of rock in our family, the last
to dig deep into the dark and to let coal dust cover his skin.

The fissures of his shovel strikes against shale and siltstone
reverberate in our lungs, crack in our ribs, crumble
into dust shavings settling at the back of our throats,
each of us still miners of the 7th Anthracite Coal District
     mapping our way under bedrock,
     reaching into dark caverns for seeds of rock,
          seeds of watershed, seeds of light
          blessing this geology of our genealogy.

SUSQUEHANNA PETROGLYPHS

       Etched into
schist and sandstone with simple stone tools
held in hands hundreds of seasons ago

Boundary markers, signals to others,
      a vocabulary of pressure against pressure,
carvings still speaking with light and water

     four serpents mark
       equinoxes

     Thunderbirds, Martens,
       humans,
          swirls,
    seven sisters constellation

You & I map the unknown,
     the foreverness of the above,
     the desire to be heard, the need to mark place,
onto the hard surface of rock that gathers us

We trace patterns of dialogue
            stretched
across estuaries, ecotones, centuries, star clusters,
       to connect to the communal
     language of lives
sheltered in shared syllables of existence.

THE RIVER, A MOUTH

for Steve

We walk the river's jaw
      along its curved bone ledges,
            long palates growing eelgrass,
                  spooking baitfish and bass, to the dam.

Rusty crayfish flick through
      summer teeth slick boulders as we slip
            the weight of our bodies becomes buoyant
                  and we float until our boots touch bottom.

Lightning bugs splatter
      shorelines as storms split us in two.
            Rain downstream, lightning upstream,
                  dam at our back, we are halves of all we held.

We wade deeper into the dark
      our feet become a bed of pebbles
            our legs tooth roots buried in bone
                  our waists eddies, our chest hair hibiscus.

We follow the river's tongue
      down its throat into its lungs
            and feel the crack of thunder choking
                  our names in the language of water and rock.

II - RIVERLAND HYMNS

Go to any place where there are more rivers than roads;
trade your flesh for any moving water
—Michael Delp

LITURGY OF CARP BECOMING A GOD

Find an island thick with knotweed
      and two white egrets stalking shallows,
wade downstream along the bank pausing every few feet
      to let the river show you how to be,
to make sure that the rocks and ledges you see
      are what they are and not what you want them to be.
Climb over the trunk of a lightning struck river birch,
      look into water, and you are still, let your eyes adjust,
find a school of seven large carp brushing their scales against sunken
      branches. Breathe until you begin to blend, slowly kneel
until knees hit soft sediment that's soaked for most of the year
      but it's August and the river is thirsty,
and these carp, they are shuffling like stalks of corn in mourning wind
      and everything moves as if we're caught in a hidden riverland hymn.
And you are still. Follow their rhythms until you notice
      they are taking turns swimming into the deep
channel to suck down little damselfly nymphs, letting water usher them
      into the shallow end of the pool where they feel it slow and scoot
quick up under the deadfall waiting their turn and your fingers
      are in the water reaching for their tails hoping to touch one
since you can't seem to land one with your fly rod
      and now your palm is wet and you brush off the memory
of a wafer turned into body amen and a long walk back to your pew
      as the next carp takes its turn you slide
your whole arm in and let it become water and you are still
      and haven't breathed in a few seconds
and you think you finally found the right words to build a prayer
      that will be heard and when you exhale they notice you,

because that's what Gods do, notice,

       and they dart off into the deep current and your
palms are left open and once sediment settles

       you consider sliding your whole body into water
to become a river-prayer-flag forever caught in current.

OYSTER RIVER LOVE SONGS

I would feed on an essence
until it yields to me my own dumb form
—Jim Harrison

Overture

Water breaks over rocks,
Sun shifts across worn hills,
Silver maples color islands,
Our feet touch water, water laps our skin.
Our eyes, they see. Our ears, they hear.

The river is the singer, the river is the creator, the river
gives us names, gives us breaths, gives us paths
—upstream, Otsego; downstream, Chesapeake—

We ferry fingers along its spine searching for a song,
for a reason, for a lover that will roll in its humid
mud that spreads our pores and burns us like stinging
nettle then kisses us calm. A melody laps into a murmur.

Song of Shad

We breathe salt for so long
that we almost choke on the clean
water at her mouth when we
finally reach it in spring.

Our bodies are built to bring
us back home, as we get closer
the hug becomes tighter, swaddled
in the banks of our mother.

That was when we filled this river
cherished, hunted, wanted.
Now we clamor at an end long before
    we are ready to sow our seed.
Now we breathe shallow brine breaths
    never tasting home.

Song of Catfish

I taste river with my skin.

Whiskers scant along bottom,
    we are the color of mud,
the color of silt, the color of burnt
    deadwood drifting down.

I taste river with my skin

I gorge on murk, where the river bends
in on itself, the dark hollows and channels
that are always deepening, always carving.

I taste river with my skin

I grind fins to speak, I flex, I drum.
Lick my skin and taste the river.
Lick my skin smoked on hot coals.
Lick my skin and let your tongue
dance to the lyrics of dolomite and diabase.

Song of Heron

A quiet stalk
        while eyes search sides.
A long sharpness
        of ice sliced by the sun.

I am a soft quiet wire brush
drawn in circles on a snare drum.

Chorus

This river feeds us
This river names us
This river chants our mantras
        Water against rock, sun on leaf,
        Wing through air, fin in current.

Song of Sycamore

My dust, my bark, my slick skin
        my tart green leaves in spring.
Hear me one last time before the floods,
Hear me sing my reclamation song.

My roots take hold
in English ivy and strewn furnace bricks.
They suck metals from dirt,
if you peel me slowly you can smell the smelting
you can feel the hot furnace, suck on my buds
and taste the sweat from the necks of men.

Song of Smallmouth

There is a place for me here.

There are minnows
                flashy darts
There are hellgrammites
                dark kernels
There are crayfish
                rusty jigs.

There is a place for me here.

My bronzeback and burnt shadows
streaking down my flanks etch this water.
        I inhale pops on the surface
        I snarl at what runs away.

Song of Cormorant

I hover
      I dive
I search
      for fish
below surface.
      My blackness
streaks air
      like arrows
shot from
      poplar limbs.

Song of Dams

A deep pool, an endless fullness
and stillness where once a ripple
and movement lived, where once
the river caressed the mouth of creeks
with its tongue, where once, in warming
days after cold days fat silvers broke through
currents looking for their birthplace and black
branches fluttered to the bay looking for salt.

      I hold, here, I hold.
I break currents, I break paths, I break.

Chorus

This river feeds us
This river names us
This river chants our mantras
     Water against rock, sun on leaf,
     Wing through air, fin in current.

Song of Solomon Seal

Arching over duff, long and slender,
little bells hang from my underside
ringing olms of understory,
whispering of lost chestnuts that stood
thick and tall above me, that cast
cooling shadows over my back, that held
me close during storms as water
trampled closer and closer.

Song of Eel

I roll rhythms just a beat behind.
They sang songs for me back when
I was caught in nets, nailed to logs, sliced
down the middle and cooked laid splayed
on top of hot coals. Back when I swam
to salt to spawn then retreated back here,
where I blend in with the zostera.

I am grass. I am the way of the current.

Song of Knotweed

I mimic small arcs below me,
        thin and fragile,
my skin like bamboo shoots that taste
        good pan fried.

I fill islands, I fill clearings,
I fill lowlands at least four feet high.
I fill what was before, a fullness forever.

Song of Carp

Mud is our home, murkiness
follows us as we swim, we tie
tight copper coils in shallows
to spawn, we tread under mulberry
trees our lips tattooed purple with juice
smearing river bottom.

Chorus

This river feeds us
This river names us
This river chants our mantras
        Water against rock, sun on leaf,
        Wing through air, fin in current.

Bridge

A low lonesome song in the summer lull
for the shade of the bank, trees it can't reach.

With rain the river bellies and slows in an eddy,
a deep bass beat of the days to come.

Storms flicker on its western edge,
stalled, watching it flow for a moment
before heading to the coast.

Song of Catalpa

There are stories of hotness
well below us. This hotness
is creeping back, I think this
is where I come from. Where
many months are wet and air
is thick with moisture.

My seed is long and slender,
like beans that creep up vines,
mine creep down a new tropical
pattern. My wood is good
smoked with eel and shad
and even catfish, now.

Song of Banks

I hold, I recede, sometimes
I stretch with drought, my rock knuckles
scorched by sun, I belly with flood,
torn docks, tires, and collapsed canoes.

I am quiet chasing the water, I am loud
losing myself to rain. I curve, I bend.
       I am an artifact
       constantly born.

Coda

Upstream, downstream,
bridges and dams. People pulse,
blood drips from hawk beards,
coal smoke streams from furnace stacks,
farmers spread manure on seeded fields
hours before the rain.

We will leave, macadam will crack,
water will flow, hills will erode, continents
will shift, the river will flow, the river will flow
singing an endless song of water over rock.

WHEN HE WAS A CUTBANK

He missed every sunset
      trying to be the perfect
           selvage of water and soil.

He knew darkness could be a house
and that life mostly erodes from below.

He saw the world as a confluence caught
constantly scraping, cracking, breaking.

He had faith in the rhizomatic marriage
                  of root and dirt
                        holding the ledge
        cradling his world.

BROOK TROUT AUBADE

When he gets these mornings,
        about once a month,
he likes to take things slow, knowing
        not much else matters,
so he drinks an extra cup of coffee
        before filling his Stanley thermos
and opening the truck door that sticks
        in the cold that still lingers
in the April morning and lets
        it warm up while the *Eat a Peach*
tape catches and hisses a bit before
        starting right in the middle
of "Mountain Jam" and he rides with
        Duane's glass pill bottle sliding strings
and finds himself at the gate of State
        Forest lands and parks and reaches
for his six-foot spinning rod already strung
        with a Panther Martin that his wife
bought him in Bozeman on their last trip out west
        when the guy behind the counter just squinted
at her under his flat brimmed hat unable
        to understand anyone not buying
a big hopper or at least a streamer but he ended
        up catching a lot of cutties that day
and never switched it out and by the time he remembers
        the last fish and its pink-slashed throat he's at the final
plunge pool before it gets too steep and he casts
        and the lure plops and he waits a second

while it sinks just a little and he begins his jigging
       retrieve and before half the line is back
he sees the red flash underbelly of a brook trout
       and he lets it dart a bit before bringing
it to his palm underwater and he considers
       how everything he's ever held
has eventually been released.

THE RIVER, A GATHERING

Feral when it floods,
nothing to do but watch it flail and fill
and wait while it takes what it wants,
pulling down the flotsam we'll dig
through for anything worth saving—
       wire, lumber, bicycles,
         shelter for the chickens.

Once Jimmy found a whole Jon boat
that we worked on all summer until
finally getting it running in September
only to have the Conservation Officer
tag us without a launch permit or registration
and they took the boat and trailer and another
time we found a bundle of glow sticks
still glowing, fading into an underwater jellyfish
rainbow stuck on sunken sycamore branches
that we'd throw rocks at trying to see who
could get the longest ripples,
       a muddy river turned into a fluorescent flag.
       Wind and water, they go still and disappear.

Back before the river, we'd go to Sunday gatherings
       —hands waving in the air, knees sinking to the ground—
and that was the last we felt that many people at once.

       In the winter it's just ice
       creaking itself into a thaw.

Once it recedes we drive upriver to each boat
launch looking, scavenging and sifting.

    All this roiling, all this tumbling,
        it all settles someday.

THE POET STUMBLES UPON A USED HYPODERMIC NEEDLE
WHILE FISHING IN SCHUYLKILL COUNTY

after Todd Davis

and quickly, finally notes how the sun has rested

    behind the hill, and how shadows of rhododendron

are now covering everything, and how the deep run underneath

    the far bank where he caught a brown trout with a brake light

red adipose fin is perfectly watched from the syringe's resting spot,

    and how this is a good place to be alone, between the railroad tracks

the river the woods the highway and the strip club and at least

    they put the cap back on and maybe they love the way this nook

feels like being somewhere-completely-else in an unrelenting

    wildness as much as he does and he wonders if this is from the guy

he saw crawl from the tent downstream behind the burnt-out hotel

    which makes him think about the economy and how there used to be jobs

around here back when these woods were rusty thin, lining factories burning

    but the darkness is getting fuller, heavier, and his truck is a ways

upstream and he no longer wants to be alone nor does he want

    to meet someone back here so he makes one last roll cast and strips

the black woolly bugger back, not even letting it jig or drift

    a bit before he reels in and wades across the stream

PENOBSCOT SUITE

I allow myself eddies of meaning
—A.R. Ammons

1

Dust, dirt, down the Golden Road,
    Abol Bridge, Penobscot River,
    Debsconeag Lakes and Salmon Point,
        I am forever returning to Katahdin's shadows.

2

A horizon of caddis, yet salmon aren't close to the surface.
    Where are they? Down, down, down.
Wet spring. 27 inches of snow on the ground in April.
One Brown Drake on the picnic table. End of June.
    I've come back upstream alone.

3

Ravens at 4:30 in the morning,
the river always a murmur,
a mouth full of consonants,
late afternoon logging trucks
barrel over gravel, cheeks of vowels.

4

The sunset shadow
moves up pine,
    light like egg
    in a cool cast iron.

5

I was young the first time
I was covered with this water.
21, I could barely grow a beard, 21
I could eat anything I liked and drink
hard those three days we had off after four tens.

I almost didn't make it, I almost got swallowed
by Jawbreaker Rapid, but somehow at the last
moment my stroke caught and I got a hold
and I was never so tired as when I pulled myself
up on that granite ledge, that slick sharp edge cutting
the middle seam of every finger, my life jacket heavy.

I felt the whole weight of my body
for the first time. I fell in love with rock.
I fell in love with this river and this mountain.
I keep coming back, trying to grab a hold.

6

Father, Son, Holy Ghost. Salmon, Cedar, Stream.
Red canoe, green slicker, Nancy's Prayer caddis.

7

How many songs can I sing?
How many mountains will I fall in love with?
How many salmon will I search for?

8

If it isn't black flies,
    it's wood smoke
            and a downpour
just as salmon start licking surface.

9

It rained last night. It's Wednesday
and I can't remember my dreams.
    The river is still there,
      the three ravens wake me up
        every morning with first light.
My dog is staring at me. The red
canoe anchors every night across the eddy.

10

Socked in, without wool warmth,
just the sweet breeze of cedar in a storm.
Just my dog and I. Is this lonesomeness? No.

Just the moose in the bog blending in with deadwood,
stumps turned over in fierceness, quietly submerging
themselves back to ground. Back to dirt.

11

I woke this morning in a bed of ache
with a bracelet of black fly bites.

Is this what getting old is?
I pissed next to an oak and watched
a chipmunk nuzzle the soft underside
of a rotting branch becoming
the silky splinters of decaying wood.

12

Splices of dream crack the chorus
of a morning mixtape from an old lover

> *I am not your Academy.*
> *I am not*
> *your Academy.*

13

Sometimes the way wood falls
furnishes fire its path to our world.

Sometimes the way birch leans
leads burnt embers to land.

Sometimes the way mountains
mend mold conifer like clay.

Each night I wait for caddis to hatch
and salmon to nudge the surface
and sometimes they do just for a moment or two
before rain and yet the red canoe stays anchored
and he keeps fishing until dark even in downpours.

14

There's a blue that comes before dark
when the sun pushes night away
that must be the closest to the color we see
right as we leave our mother's womb.

15

Sometimes I put on the longest version
of "Old Strange" and let it fill my lungs,
breathing into a trance as Gunn's guitar
threads itself into a mysterious mantra,
a reverence of following and finding.

                                 Hallelujah.

16

My dog and I take baths in smoke,
the same kind our mothers
would have given us had they known
the sacred ways of Wood and Water.

Smoke soothes our bites.
Smoke lifts our eyes.
Smoke cleanses our tongues
          Shows us air, guides our breaths.

17
I pray in the eddy,
          swirl of psalm
          flotsam of faith
          cast of communion
          genuflection of grace.
Hands clasped, head bowed, eyes closed.

18
Tracing outlines of old memories
in sweet smoke of soft fir, land laid
on, nights slept under, reliving memories
from 15 years ago.

These stars and storms
and wind that clear the palette of bugs
are new, they are not of then, but of now.

It's easy to get caught in a tangled monofilament knot of the past,
sometimes, usually, it's best to just cut it and start tying again.

19
A long black slice through pink
feldspar granite, a seam.
Water over a ledge,
          is that you?
No, just another island of alder.

20

This river takes my dreams
I do not remember them—
      are they drowned?
      caught in the dead water?
      roiling into each other for a salt song I cannot sing?

Maybe they become their own estuary
        a briny mixture
of fear doubt sex old love, rain, cormorants, sap,
thunder that pinches eyelids, brake lights, lightning bugs.

21

An old man slouches in a red canoe
     every night, river left.
Every few minutes, he puffs a cigarette,
casts only when he feels he should—not like
the rest of us, ceaselessly drawing streaks through the air,
      constantly searching, moving.
He waits, lets it come to him. Watches.

22

It is raining now
     will rain again,
The hatch has ended,
     the salmon aren't rising,
we may go back
     but we can never relive.

23

How long has that old man been slouched
in that red canoe? Each night, though in the same
place, must be an entirely new awakening.
He can mark his days well, with life lived.

He doesn't think of his dreams.
He doesn't think about returning.
He is here.

24

Deliberate casts, studied water, he lets storm clouds
pass over his rain jacket, a clear haze of cigarette smoke.

A buddha in a red canoe.

25

We must honor totems
        of life lived
we must bow, we must sing
we must tip our drinks to them.
                A toast.

26

Buddha in a red canoe
waits every night for what he knows
will happen and what will happen
may only happen for a few minutes
but he honors that happening,
he eddies in a place of reverence
where he devotes his life
to what he loves.

27
The way the sun
reaches water
blinds me.

28
The salmon,

                    return

                    every year.

The caddis,

                    hatch

                    every summer.

29
Devote our lives
to what we love.

30
       We come back
into different water (Penobscot),
into different shadows (Ktaadn),
into different dreams (cedar).

CASTING FROM A CANOE

based on a sketch by Richard Harrington

This is the balance of being we seek—
casting a fly rod while standing in a canoe.

Our shadow wavers in the back cast,
water slowly laps on wood until the fly
settles in its full reach on a riffle, a murmur
we wish to translate into a knowing, a holding.

We find this balance as we float
              —searching, watching, waiting.

CONRAD, PENNSYLVANIA 8:20 PM

for Scot, Andy, & Kurt

Sulphurs, Green Drakes, Alders
hug water like moths smother light.

Brook trout rise to bugs dropping
         eggs on the water's skin.
The moon pulls in the Milky Way.

What gods do we pray to in moments like these?

Those of our dead fathers and yellow stoneflies?
Those of thorn scratches across shins,
tattoos from thick hollows and watershed elders
chanting their ancient songs in the deepest plunge pools?

These long prayers hold together with last light
cascading off clouds rhyming with curves of hills.

HOPPER JUNCTION GHAZALS

for Rick, Ann, & Justin

1.

Glaciers once scraped this land and in that steady recession
left a sea slowly pulled north into a series of lakes and streams.

We stand in a cold swamp, a sandy once-ocean-once-lake-bottom,
caught in a centuries-long low tide, an unfurling of a water floor.

Yarrow, horsemint, great crested flycatchers, eastern wood pewees.
Let us name the grains of this land that were uncovered by the melt.

Perhaps if we stand here long enough, we'll become water once again.
Perhaps if we lie in the river long enough, we will taste the old sea.

Perhaps in watching cedar waxwings careen from alder to alder
we learn flight and will meet in the air, where fish once swam.

2.

Birds stitch air where fish once swam,
our bodies recede back into their water.

The downstream riverbend's concave bow
shows us how to accept this inevitable eroding.

In that erosion, deep pools hold salmon returning
home to their water cradle—thin and taut headwaters.

Only in water do we notice how deadwood stacks
in the dark of a bend giving a sandy bank stability.

Bee balm and Queen Anne's lace, fields of bracken fern,
white oak. Let us lie here and watch forest reclaim ocean.

3.

Only in water do we feel hidden
currents land creates with its creases.

Only in water do we see a stonefly
scuttle along the underside of a rock.

Only in water do we feel hardpan
shift and crumble under our weight.

Only in water do woodland bluffs become
streamside songs sung sinking into riverbed.

Only in water do we discover how our bodies
shape this world, how the unseen sews the seen.

III - BLOOD & BARK

The river is a river again
—Jill Osier

THE RIVER, DARK

We walk the tracks in the dark
with a six pack and lit Camel Lights
as flashlights and bug dope, chicken livers
and sharp hooks jostle in tackle boxes, down to the abandoned
mill—Billmyer—and the quarry, its quartz swimming pool blue
water held back by rock. We sit on the white cliff culm piles
and say we are fishing for catfish but just smoke a whole pack
and get a buzz from cheap beer.

Sometimes I think we are still sitting, smoke
melding the night to our fingers and lips.

Sometimes I think that we went there in a dream
that is still living in the sleeping body of our youth.

Sometimes I think we fell in love with a dark river,
turning our backs to the dawn, keeping its faint orange spread
in the corner of our eyes, watching it chase our gods under water.

SHAD WARS

When the river runs without rain and waves roll
like wooden barrels down Front Street stuttering
across brick, we pull out pitchforks and nets
and wade into the Susquehanna to meet shad.

These past few years have been tough, just a few hauls
before it's only eels tangled in nets. We have to sneak downriver
at night to Columbia ever since they built weirs as tall as pig iron
furnaces to funnel water into the canal, keeping shad pooled
under the bridge lit with candles and mayflies
        —haloes of greedy saints.

Word is those Conestoga folk down at the Mason-Dixon
line built zigzagging rock dams that trap those silver mallets
and pushes them nose-to-nose flailing right into their nets.
I hear some Columbia folk got full-on drunk and hiked down
the raftman's path hoping to bust those rock walls and cut
        some seine nets only to stare into
        the black moon of a Griffin cannon.

We'll keep watching for those waves,
        for the river to breathe and as those breaths
            get shallower and the dams bigger
                we'll wade further and further.

FISHING PENNS CREEK DURING A PANDEMIC

Go ahead and let the world change—
I'm happy to sit among these cliffs.
—Han Shan

Spruce pine hemlock,
       thick around river,
peel back curtains
       of red buds draped
on hillsides. It's still early spring.

Black stoneflies and blue winged olives
       flit in that liminal moment
between sky and water. Brown trout
       nose the surface seining and swallow
emergers reaching their next life.

I spread nothing but casts across water
       in a lockdowned world I stare into space
where hunger and desire meet asking for a response,
       waiting for the next metamorphosis.

ASHLAND

on a note from Nana

"The town of Ashland
      is almost completely abandoned
because of the gases coming up
      from the old mine.

Many years later they are still coming up"

Maybe we live on a rock balloon
and all these punctures are slow leaks
and soon we collapse, a crumbling
deflation of sediment schist shale
all the rock all the fossils all the detritus
and death of billions of years and lives
and when empty we aimlessly flap around the solar
system losing our orbit like dried November
leaves until a burst strong and quick
breaks the last of us into tiny little pieces
floating and falling into the punctures
of the universe, filling space, gathering
into a new world built on the abandoned
towns impaled by our lust for light.

BULLY PULPIT

Conestoga Massacre, December 1763

Reverend Elder preached at the pulpit
with a rifle in one hand, a bible in the other

    that they were good men in private,
        they heard his sermons, got drunk, went downstream
    they were virtuous and respectable,
        they found the Susquehannock at daybreak
    they were not cruel or mean, no,
        they scalped and killed and burnt their homes
    they were mild and they were merciful
        the survivors were put in the local jail

the barrel always angled up to his heaven,
tracing the oak rafters in its crosshairs
as he slammed psalms and scripture
down with his fist into the hard
backs of his pews and his congregation
as his Lord & Rifle Cloak shook

    these Paxton Boys were men that tilled their land
        for protection from the Paxton Boys
    that only wanted to protect their family and their God
        but two days after Christmas
    that simply rode the storm that had been gathering
        they broke in and found 14 taking refuge

for quite some time just like anyone else would
      they chased down families with Tomahawks
they wished not to be taken by the thunder
      they split heads, scalped, cut off hands and feet
and lightning but to give it, to control it.
      and then finally a bullet in each mouth.

with praises of the Almighty, Amen.

RUST BELT OSSUARY

This fractured land holds me with its coal dust
clinging to everything—casting gray shades,
oily coffee sheen. Brittle metal crust
crumbling between fingers is just decades
      of moonsets behind smokestacks and beer cans
      floating in jackknifed rivers of sewage.
           I wade deep in the salvage of farm lands
           draining field-sediment tainted fluids.
I drank the creek and thought it was its blood;
I swallowed and fell in love with water
      and its wakes—prayers coiled, roiling floods
      hurling my bent body into boulders
coming to rest in stained estuaries
bleeding from these rust belt ossuaries.

POST-INDUSTRIAL WILDERNESS, REJOICE!

I propose a Post-Industrial Wilderness designation
        where we sing hymns of abandoned
        collieries slowly decaying into rocky
        soil strewn with concrete and shovels.

Let us call these corrugated hillsides *Wilderness*
        Let us rejoice in rust!

Let us rejoice in the stutter step cadence
        of walking rail ties leading into headwaters
        trickling out of mine shafts covered by hemlock.
Let us place limestone back into the water,
        an offering of reclamation.

Let us praise this river that was killed and is burnt
orange but thriving with wild trout and midges fluttering
above oily sheen and its life, its resilience, its wildness
returning and spreading and all its tarnished beauty!

Let us bulldoze dams and let water run wild again.
Let it grow, all of it, even the invasives.
Let knotweed arc over thistle and beer can.
        For what is native in a place that has been
        scraped and curled by furnace blasts?

Let us lie in the debris of our consumption
and smile when we feel worms between our toes,
glass shard pushing into the back of our calf,

a plastic lid crinkling under our fourth rib
a cement wall in the kink of our neck
a fleck of neon light that never stops
shimmering in our eyelash.

Let the earth swear at us
Let us love these curse words
Let them become sacred lines, holy
        prayers healing the cracks of our destruction.
Let us rejoice in the off-key harmony
        of mountain laurel and anthracite.

Let us rename this slag heap with signs
marking the boundaries of the abandoned:

        Post-Industrial Wilderness
            Rejoice!

LYING IN A HAMMOCK WITH WICKED WIND COMING OFF THE ANDROSCOGGIN RIVER

for my mother

A white pine embraces a dead oak branch
rubbing it as wind shakes off the river
like sheets snapped dry on a clothesline.

Tall grass and garlic gone feral covers my periphery,
body blurs into cloth, my belly button brings memories
of my mother buying me a Skeletor action figure from K-Mart

     I was holding it out the window while she drove
     so it could fly but the wind was too strong
          for my little fingers and it flew
     and for a moment I was captured by magic witnessed
          but then quickly cried when I felt
     all that wind in my hand pushing my fingers
     straight and she turned the car around and searched the tall
     grass and gravel along the road and finally bent down and reached
     under a guardrail and brought the purple hooded plastic humanoid
     still clutching his sword and Havoc Staff back as cars swooshed by.

That dead branch will break and the pine will grow,
its mark fading into each year's rings like how I hold
     my mother in the balance of my body
     always buoyed in my center

WHEN HE WAS A DRAG QUEEN

for Cameron//Carrington. With so much love.

He lost his name in glitter gods
sparkling over every fucking
thing and finally felt her chest
take a full breath reveling
the tension of skin against strap
the balance of heels on hardwood
and her voice became a song
smearing lipstick harmonies
across bar tops and subway
tiles and her wig cradled her head
her back arched in joy and her eyes
hoped you knew how much she loved you.

STURGEON MOON

An osprey sweeps thin the sky above us,
   a dead native fallfish splayed across rocks.
We interrupted dinner dragging plastic
   kayaks against river bottom, with
stumbling cursing grunts through shallow water.

This would be worth it if the bass were biting
   like they should be. But they're not.
Neither are the sturgeon since they are gone from these waters.
   Dams, chemical sprays, lawns, macadam, non-natives.
We don't belong, yet here we are
   celebrating the moon and waters
   that are still named by ancestors,
   the ones-here-first, or maybe second.

I like this not knowing
   the distinct lines
between native, wild, invasive.

   I gather in this blur of identity
   and become a star only seen
   after a heavy rain in the Badlands on a new moon
   night, clay saturated, steps thick and heavy, Milky
   Way stretched quietly across the butte.
         Here I am

   still grunting, feet still in water,
   dragging a kayak across rock,
   watching an osprey, looking for bass.

COAL COUNTRY BROOK TROUT: A MEMOIR

I find myself on the edge of a bank eroding into rushing
water—layers of clay, schist, and sandstone
compressed into a cake sandwiching black curves of

       Peacock coal
Anthracite too beautiful to burn

ragged hymns of black diamond eyes
       flickering in full moons,
the Morse code of brook trout halos

which I follow into long slow pools that I want
to rush over to get to the fast riffles quicker
where the flows force into each other and
water folds in on itself before roiling
into deep laughing sighs and I sink
into that joyful susurrus and nestle
streambed rock rustling out
caddis, stonefly, the native
speckles of these
tight veins.

LITURGY OF BECOMING AN ERRATIC

Find yourself under soft soil following loam fibers folding
and fashioning you as coldness steadily recedes, a thaw
that becomes a womb buoying you above the branched
reach of this seep, keep still while the frigid warms
into a comforting freshet that finally exposes you.

      Even without lungs air and light move

Watch as bugs flit in it. Read it. Anticipate its cursive.
Once you understand, clouds and rains will come—
      Fall in the fluting as you find your footing.

You will be scratched and pressed and held
and stripped naked and in that nakedness
      —friction, sound—
you stand and spread and scatter
slowly and create a cocoon of roaring.

You shapeshift shadows into deep pools
Your voice is your stillness, is how
You and water sculpt each other

      You hold a river.

FATHER JOE

maybe the greatest miracle is memory
—Brian Doyle

The holiest moments
were those curse words
Father Joe muttered under
his breath when some *asshole*
walked down the aisle or when, *shit,*
the choir started in too early. I always
volunteered to sit on his right so I could
hold the Bible open leaned in against my
sternum, *Jesus Christ,* as he read the Liturgy of the Word.
He'd gently, *damnit,* slide the long tassels across the pages
like a blessing. I still follow his eyes as he reads, arms
bent up from his elbows tucked into his side, palms up
Glory Be to the Highest, *sonofabitch,* listening
for those curse words in that sacred syntax.

COLD MOON BIRTHDAY GHAZAL

The sky is everywhere, always light and dark breaching
the skin of this world, eyes forever opening and reaching.

Tonight, the final full moon stretches to its apsis,
straddling the earth in its winter reaching.

The frozen pond is still, yet under that settling-surface-silent
knowing that to-reach is to never-hold is water always reaching.

I was born on this day, at the year's hinge of past and future,
cast into a life of in-between, constantly settling and reaching.

There are times when I am sure of my faith in the unseen,
when my bicycle leans me into the comfort of all this reaching.

There are times when I only see the water in front of me
yielding to downstream dams slowly stalling its reaching.

There are times when I can't remember how old I am,
lost in bright sunlight torrents beating branches, reaching.

My name is stubborn, a moon listening for the pond's teaching,
a horizon holding sound and syllables caught in all this reaching.

SKITTERING CADDIS

for Andrew Gottlieb

Casting a caddis to a rattlesnake rhythm,
landing it upstream of a riverbend,
it floats in the current break as sun carves
hickory leaves into an amber nimbus.

Water brings line tight
                                        skittering
                        the
                caddis
from a deep undercut bank
            across riffles into an abrupt
                        —pause—
a knife slicing an apple from stem to stamen.

When tension of
            line fly water light
                        meet
a brook trout lifts off riverbed
takes the fly the sky and all
its clouds and even the breeze
that these tight hollows harken
and cuts quick downstream to a hemlock
deadfall until I nudge him and bring him
to the shallows and hold him in water and
release him from hook and finally, everything
sighs, tension gone, the water on my
knees cools the rattler quiets and the trout
flashes and we go silent and turn upstream.

MATING AUBADE

She likes to count the birds at the feeder each morning
so she doesn't lose track of the seasons, which is easy to do

when you are unmoored, adrift, when sometimes snow
doesn't mean winter and sun doesn't mean summer,

and she's lost in this no-place until he turns over and wakes up
always with dawn light and she hears their dog stretch and shake

and she's back, here, not there, not longing, not holding emptiness
which only sinks you or lets you float away—an anchor or sail. Seven.

This morning there are seven birds: three thrushes, two warblers,
two cardinals—a mating pair of bright red & pale brown.

She follows their darting flight to their nest of twigs
and spotted eggs to make sure the cats can't get them.

WHERE EELS SPAWN HAIBUN

For years no one knew where eels went to spawn once they left their rivers. For years they disappeared. For years they simply vanished then reappeared as small slivers sliding back into their freshwater homes. Finally, someone tracked one and found them in the Sargasso Sea where the four Atlantic currents collide—the Gulf Stream from the east, the Canary from the west, the North Atlantic and Equatorial from the North and South—and drop the detritus of their land, clockwise, growing into a clear blue ocean graveyard gyre of seaweed and eel. I bet you could find the DNA of every living thing in that sea. Something died, something ate it, something decomposed, water came, washed it to sea. Eels spawn where our deaths lie, bringing us back when they return to our rivers.

Held in these currents,
We are maps of each other,
a shared water faith.

IV - CONCLUDING RITES

Somehow it has all
added up to song
—Wendell Berry

THE RIVER, A GHOST

Bones break water—vertebrae tracing sky
no longer womb but a large eddy that never dries,

its depth and darkness a kindness on summer days,
the river giving birth in its slow dissolve into a ghost.

Each day hotter than the last disappears another droplet
until, slowly, our eyes adjust and we notice its descent.

Soon it's all we can tell of the river, what it used to be, what it used to cover.
We are left with narrow straps of water flesh, taut ligaments too thin to hide fish,

thin enough that a heron only needs to swoop close to break surface,
a puncture of proximity that we wish we could fully feel,

for if we could we would bleed out from so many beak stabs,
glorious in their precision and sharpness, so sure of themselves.

In that river's absence we are given a new topography,
a new horizon to follow as light reaches and recedes.

This is what we follow. And this is how I want to end this drought
recitation, but this is bullshit, metaphor only goes so far.

I am sorry for turning another river into another metaphor,
for hiding grief when I know full-well that to hide is to bury,

for trying to compare a river in drought
to a couple unable to have children.

It is never memory, just haunting in the periphery
a shadow we can never quite trace back to its solid form.

Can something never alive become a ghost?

We once believed in subterranean streams seeping,
reclaiming rivers, a conjuring of hope into life.

In the slow fade, rock is all we touch.
We are left with river bones.

And this is also bullshit. Here.

We are left with desire for rain.
We are left with sunlight and moonlight and nights so dark
        all we are is thigh against thigh
        all we hear is the slow murmur of water kissing rock
        all we trace is the intertwining of our ligaments,
            liturgies of love, a topography
so thin so taut we can't help but break
our ghosts into pieces with our thirst.

LITURGY OF GOING TO WATER

Everything relies on everything else in order to manifest
—Thich Nhat Hanh

We hike the owl's crown down to an old burn that runs its way
        into a confluence of muddy currents and knotweed.
Cast, turn, trace the ravine back to its narrowest point
        flicking Royal Wulffs, studying scat, naming plants,
fingers reach riverbed through speckled sediment shadows,
        an interbeing of brook trout and body manifesting
landscape lineages of what we seek, marbled watersheds
        emptying and returning, always, to another river.

for Todd & Noah

TWO CATHOLICS MEET OVER A CAMPFIRE

The guilt is always there, isn't it?
                    a pink sky brushes the Androscoggin

                                        I even rang bells and wore robes.
                    a loon call creases our cheeks

But it was the way they lined up,
                                                        Yes!

to eat that silly wafer
                                                        right?

And I remember asking, wait, is this really his body?
                                                        Yes!

yes, they said.

                        You know, that's a beautiful thing, isn't it?
                        something that shouldn't need a line or robe.

            she stares at fire collapsing wood

                        My favorite part was always after when
                        everyone shook hands and said
                        "Peace be with you,"
                        "and also with you."

            we brush mosquitoes off our arms

I loved moving around the pews searching
for hands to hold, taking the body.
I miss that.

                                                        Yes.

WHEN HE WAS A CHINOOK SALMON

based on "Chinook Salmon Woodcut" by Richard Harrington

He grew a ridge of mountains
        along the edges of his mouth
as he kissed freshwater for the first
        time since he was a smolt.

His gums grew dark, his hook sharp,
        his back ridged
as he worked his way home listening
        to that dark voice behind his gill plate.

His salt scars stretch, scratched above
        his lateral line horizon,
as his mouth gulps and his caudal fin
        digs gravel beds for his seed.

He lies in shallow still water waiting
        for the bear he hears lumbering
along the bank, trying to finish the song started
        here, years ago, before he arrives,

        His world mapped on his skin.

RIVERLANDS AUBADE

The river is always there
even when he doesn't see it for weeks
because he's busy milking cows and scooping
pig shit and piling fieldstone into a wall
along the low end of their property,

—something to slow erosion,
      something to make it all last
           a bit longer—

and his dog gets enough exercise running through the barn
and his Farmall tractor needs a new clutch
so he just glances at the pond and watches water
trickle from the outlet into the creek that reaches
for a few hundred yards downstream
and convinces himself he can hear the river's song.

      It's always there.

When he watches sunlight land on the trees
touching them like they want to be touched, lightly,
he's comforted knowing this river will take him *someday*
and he hopes it's a morning like this, after he's had some coffee
and he's awake, sharp, after lingering in the symphony of breaths
from his wife and dog lying beside each other in their bed,
the warmth and life of that union clinging to his arms
so he has something comforting to hold
as he sinks wide-eyed and open-mouthed
into the deepest channel that runs
along the opposite bank.

THE POET SITS ON A LEDGE AND WRITES A LETTER

Dear Reader,

Up on Tussey Mountain I sit on rock ledges and watch windmills across the valley spin wind that reaches me shortly. I am here to tell you about the valley floor and forests turning color and fields being cut for last harvest and two bald eagles that sweep so close to me I can see feathers pulse and how I can't get the news up here but I know the world is turning by distant trains and the hum of traffic on Route 45 and how the sun is about to pull the moon into its rightful place low in the sky right next to Mars.

I am here to tell you, Dear Reader, that the river never stops flowing. Even when in drought and it's merely a trickle, the rocks move light into shadows, eddies of darkness and riffles of moss murmur low love songs. There is always a river.

I am here to tell you about the God I met along this ridge of the Allegheny Front. It caught me listening for crickets in winter. And this God ate the peanut m&ms out of the trail mix, ignoring the raisins. And this God sat with me and we said nothing and the clouds covered the forest and everything began to float and I swear the air tasted like chicken pot pie and potato rolls and we were full and in that fullness we napped.

I dreamt that we knew each other, you and I, and in that knowing words became bitter and thoughts became leaves crunching under the hooves of a buck scaling this steep ridge on opening day of archery season not seeing us, you and I Dear Reader, sitting on this ledge above him and in that unknowing, another God was formed. A question that spreads like a wool blanket over us so thickly we cannot fully wake and so we dream, you and I and that God and that buck, we dream because if we stop the river will still keep running and the rain will still come and we will miss rock turn shadows into light and we will miss moss riffles thicken with water. We will miss the mud. We will miss the eagles.

I woke from that nap so quickly I felt the world start.

I am here to tell you, Dear Reader, that all the gods I ever met have been on the edges of this world, on ledges and ridges, on thin fir needles, on foam lines of water against bank, in that granular heaven where rock and dirt meet to create *land*, where hands meet thighs to create *touch*, where light meets seed to create *life*.

Dear Reader, please know,
Every edge is an altar
in this world of ours.

RIVER THEOLOGY

written along the Middle Fork of the Flathead, for all rivers.

This was once a sea until algae breathed an atmosphere
that now cradles us in a valley of billion-year-old Belt Rock
      holding first and last light, larch and alder, grizzly and deer,
      Yarrow and Lupine, a river rippling the last waves of that ocean,
          writing the scripture of glaciers on stone
          stained the color of this ravine's birth ritual.

I sit on a ledge where a dam was to be built—
      creating a make-believe ocean that would never
      recede, swallowing, bloating into a gray mirror
stillness drowning the maps of our makings—

      and am grateful for concrete never poured and watch
      water gather joy like Red Sky Mountain gathers light,

      and read deadwood stretched across the islet
      trying to translate this year's spring-flood gospel

and rejoice in joining this wilderness congregation,
a sinuous fellowship of faith in the next bend, of following
      the downstream mystery and desire to do something
      as radical as flow over rock, swirling life into forest-at-night
          deep pools of Bull Trout ghosts and Cutthroats
          slicing erratics into a river theology

            shaping our path through this land,
            sculpting us as we return to sea.

ANOINTMENT

Arrowleaf balsamroot brushes ankles golden
      as we switchback
           down across the Yellowstone over
      two hillocks of sage
through a notch of fir and pine to where waters meet.

We wash off five-day dirt and thousands of miles of blacktop,
      Crossing ourselves, thumb on forehead mouth heart,
on a beach made from volcanic murmurs
      with sediment from an ancient eruption.

Elk antlers lay starched white in alders from spring run-off.

Stonefly husks cling to rock, their full body flutter fills the gorge,
      we wade in the riverbed reds, blues, and grays.
I could paint my life with these colors and be content dying as they dry.

      A few false casts, a cutthroat trout at the surface, a bent rod.

Where does our sediment end?
Where does it fall, gather, become
      a new piece of land, a lip of an eddy?
Will we become another, together,
when water slows enough for us to settle?

PATRON SAINT

I fell in love with arrows
piercing Saint Sebastian's taut chest,
      blood stain tattoos,
arms tied tight behind the tree
      —a reverse hug.

At Confirmation, it was God
who kept Sebastian alive
      —a bandage of belief.

Now I think it was the skin of a stone pine
that saved him, that sealed his wounds,
that cradled him into sainthood,

      a miracle of blood and bark.

BENEDICTION

All our water songs evaporate
       All our water songs evaporate
              All our water songs evaporate
                            Amen.

Acknowledgments & Notes

I am incredibly grateful to the editors of the following journals and publications in which these poems first appeared, sometimes in slightly different form. Thank you for giving them their first home.

About Place Journal - "Ashland"

Appalachia - "Liturgy of Going to Water"

Appalachian Review - "The Poet Stumbles Upon a Used Hypodermic Needle While Fishing in Schuylkill County"

Chautauqua - "Where Eels Spawn Haibun"

Eastern Iowa Review - "Upon Hearing that Snakehead Catfish Passed through the Conowingo Dam Fish Ladder"

EcoTheo - "Father Joe"

The Flyfish Journal - "Anointment"

Flyfishing & Tying Journal - "Fishing Penns Creek During a Pandemic," "Skittering Caddis"

Grist: A Journal of the Literary Arts - "Rust Belt Ossuary"

The Hopper - "Coal Country Paradise"

Louisiana Literature - "Coal Country Brook Trout: A Memoir," "Conrad, Pennsylvania, 8:20 p.m."

North American Review - "Hopper Junction Ghazals"

Northern Appalachian Review - "Dead Water Deities," "Post-Industrial Wilderness, Rejoice!"

Orange Blossom Review - "Riverlands Aubade"

Peatsmoke Journal - "Mating Aubade"

Pine Mountain Sand & Gravel: Appalachian Witness - "7th Anthracite Coal District of Pennsylvania"

Presence: A Journal of Catholic Poetry - "Searching the Database of Priests Accused of Sexual Assault"

Reimagining Magazine - "Two Catholics Meet over a Campfire"

Rewilding: Poems for the Environment - "Sturgeon Moon"

Ruminate - "Communion"

Rust + Moth - "The River, Dark"

The Shore - "The River, a Mouth"

Swing the Fly - "Learning to Spey Cast"

Tahoma Literary Review - "Liturgy of Carp Becoming a God"

Talking River Review - "The Poet Sits on a Ledge and Writes a Letter"

Water-Stone Review - "The River, a Ghost"

The Wayfarer - "Of Blood & Bark," "When He Was a Chinook Salmon"

"River Theology" was printed as a limited-edition broadside made available through The Bob Marshall Wilderness Foundation (with all proceeds going to their Artist Residency Program).

Reverend Elder's sermon in "Bully Pulpit" was paraphrased from: Sprague, William Buell (1858). *Annals of the American Pulpit: Presbyterian.* 1859. Robert Carter & Brothers. pp. 77–79.

"Penobscot Suite" contains a lyric from "Academy Fight Song" by Mission of Burma.

"On a Line from Arbouretum's 'Oceans Don't Sing'" is from the chapbook Songenizios — Poems Inspired by Songs co-written with Andrew Jones which is an adapted form from Kim Addonizio's "sonnenzio."

"Oceans Don't Sing" was released on Arbouretum's album *Coming Out of the Fog* (Thrill Jockey, 2013).

"Listenin' to Charlie Parr While Watching the Sunset Over the Middle Fork of the Flathead River" contains a lyric from "Rain" by Charlie Parr from his incredible album *Last of the Better Days Ahead* (Smithsonian Folkways Recordings, 2021).

GRATITUDE

Thank you to my family for all your love and support.

To Todd & Noah Davis for the friendship, the best writing workshops I could ever ask for, and long hikes through ravines in search of native trout.

Todd, thank you for your mentorship, for fishing behind decommissioned nuclear reactors with me, and for believing in my work.

Noah, thank you for the letters, for always being there to hear a good fishing story, and for that cutthroat along that ledge in the Anaconda Pintler Wilderness.

To Chris LaTray and the FreeFlow Institute for reminding me to "slow down, go deep, go alone."

To Geffrey Davis for urging me to write poems that promise I'll be here tomorrow.

To Andy, Scot, and Kurt for Wild Boy Run.

To Steve Mohr. Thanks brother.

To Justin Steiner for those night rides along the three rivers of Pittsburgh where I first fell in love with confluences.

To Rick Denbeau for my first backpacking pack and guiding me out into the wilderness way back when.

To Matt Gay for giving me the space to grow as a teacher and writer. I am forever grateful for the opportunities you have given me and for the encouragement and friendship. Thanks boss.

To Jeff DeBellis for offering thoughtful feedback on an early draft and for being one of the first people to share a fire in the backcountry with me.

To Angela Dribben for nudging this collection along, hearing its voices, and pulling its threads.

To Jory Mickelson for all the letters, spending time with this collection in various stages, and asking great questions.

To Justin Mando for giving me spaces to share my work. I'm grateful for our friendship sprung from the Susquehanna, defined by its watershed.

To Andrew Jones for the collaboration, feedback, encouragement, and endless texts about music. I'm so grateful our paths crossed and I can't wait to see some live music with you.

To Richard Harrington for your sketches and the long-distance collaboration.

Thanks to the following people for being part of a larger writing community that pushes, supports, and inspires me: Ryan Brod, L.M. Browning, Chris Camuto, Michael Delp, Chris Dombrowski, Elizabeth Garrigan-Byerly, Crystal Gibbins, Andrew Gottlieb, Henry Hughes, Tom & Glinda Johnson-Medland, Tyler Truman Julian, Dan Rice, Cameron Keller Scott, Anne Haven McDonnell, Sean Prentiss, Joe Wilkins, Corrie Williamson.

I am incredibly grateful for the folks that sponsor the Artist-Wilderness-Connection Program—Swan Valley Connections, the Bob Marshall Wilderness Foundation, the Hockaday Museum of Art, and the Flathead National Forest—for selecting me as an Artist-in-Residence for The Bob Marshall Wilderness in 2021 which gave me access to an incredible wilderness to explore and a place to work on this manuscript.

And finally, thank you to Jessica for building a life together where we sometimes stare out at a frozen pond for days and other times yearn for each other from faraway places, for letting me go off on wilderness adventures, for being honest, for believing in me, for digging in the dirt with me. Thank you, love.

ABOUT THE AUTHOR

Michael Garrigan writes and teaches along the Susquehanna River in Pennsylvania. He loves exploring the riverlands with a fly rod and the Pennsylvania wilds with his wife, Jess, and their dog, Whitman. He enjoys watching water move over rocks and feels strongly that every watershed should have a Poet Laureate. He was the 2021 Artist in Residence for The Bob Marshall Wilderness Area and the recipient of the Shippensburg University's Outstanding Teacher Award. Michael is the author of multiple poetry collections including *Robbing the Pillars*, and his writing has appeared in *Orion Magazine*, *Gray's Sporting Journal*, *River Teeth*, *The FlyFish Journal*, *Water~Stone Review*, *North American Review*, and *The Hopper Magazine*.

You can read more of his work at www.mgarrigan.com.

HOMEBOUND
PUBLICATIONS

Since 2011 We are an award-winning independent publisher striving to ensure that the mainstream is not the only stream. More than a company, we are a community of writers and readers exploring the larger questions we face as a global village. It is our intention to preserve contemplative storytelling. We publish full-length introspective works of creative non-fiction, literary fiction, and poetry.

Look for Our Imprints Little Bound Books, Owl House Books, *The Wayfarer Magazine,* Wayfarer Books & Navigator Graphics

WWW.HOMEBOUNDPUBLICATIONS.COM

WAYFARER

BASED IN THE BERKSHIRE MOUNTAINS, MASS.

The Wayfarer Magazine. Since 2012, *The Wayfarer* has been offering literature, interviews, and art with the intention to inspires our readers, enrich their lives, and highlight the power for agency and change-making that each individual holds. By our definition, a wayfarer is one whose inner-compass is ever-oriented to truth, wisdom, healing, and beauty in their own wandering. *The Wayfarer's* mission as a publication is to foster a community of contemplative voices and provide readers with resources and perspectives that support them in their own journey.

Wayfarer Books is our newest imprint! After nearly 10 years in print, *The Wayfarer Magazine* is branching out from our magazine to become a full-fledged publishing house offering full-length works of eco-literature!

Wayfarer Farm & Retreat is our latest endeavor, springing up the Berkshire Mountains of Massachusetts. Set to open to the public in 2025, the 15-acre retreat will offer workshops, farm-to-table dinners, off-grid retreat cabins, and artist residencies.

CPSIA information can be obtained
at www.ICGtesting.com
Printed in the USA
BVHW020247170223
658462BV00001B/4

9 781956 368376